# SAMANTA ANGELO

# THE LIGHT OF SILVER LINING WE CARRY

*Mastering the Power of Change To Transform Your Life*

# Contents

# 1

# Introduction

No matter where you are in your life, You Can be Better! Discover the potential within you and surpass your level of excellence and achievement by igniting your inner spark and making small shifts in your life.

Unlock your potential, build energy, enthusiasm, strengthen relationships and move to the next level focusing the attention on:

- Opportunities, NOT Problems
- Strengths, NOT Weaknesses
- What You CAN Do, NOT What You CAN'T

The light of silver lining you carry is the power of change: the ability each and every one of us possesses to take control of life, no matter what challenges may come on our way!

In this book, you will learn how to:

- Shift your perspective from one of scarcity to one of abundance.

You will walk through the process of identifying the things in your life that are already working well and how they can help you create even more abundance.

- Use past successes as a springboard for future progress by taking advantage of your assets and turning them into opportunities for growth and change.
- Shift your focus from what needs fixing to what works well right now, use your time in a way that builds confidence instead of anxiety!
- Look at all sides of an issue and find ways to make things better for yourself and those around you.
- Learn how to think about situations differently, you'll be able to see new opportunities, new solutions, and ultimately a new way forward for yourself.
- Focus on what you want instead of what's holding you back.

Sometimes, being affected by a crisis can push you into re-evaluating your life. The light of silver lining is a chance to re-evaluate.

By mastering the power of change you will learn in each section this book how to:

- Shift time from past to present and improve your live.
- Extract your emotional self from a situation, seeing the world-gain perspective, standing in and being aware of the moment using the past, understanding the present and looking forward.
- Achieve the perspective necessary for valid judgment and good decisions.
- Use life building blocks to recognize obstacles, learn life skills and see options for day by day life.
- Use strategy-idea to accomplish goals and tools to see the big picture

such as listening to Universe Voice, determine crucial skills and have a positive attitude.

- Understand interactions which include knowing that behavior you can control is your own; reinforce positive to achieve satisfying interactions.

You are well on your way to pursue the benefits of power of change!

Get ready for the rush of energy, and see the light that lies in a Silver Lining:

- Learn that there is always hope
- Be more grateful for what you have
- Live a happier and more fulfilling life

# 2

# Magnify Best. Focus on Next

Have you ever felt like you were stuck in the past unable to move forward? The Light of Silver Lining will help you learn how to master the change of your mindset and shift focus from past to present so that you can get unstuck and improve your life.

Change will no longer be a burden; instead, it can become an opportunity for growth and personal evolution.

You know what the best thing about the future is? It's coming.

That's right, the future is always coming. We're always moving forward, and that's a good thing! But it also means we can't stay stuck in the past.

The past is just that: something that happened before now. And if you're still holding on to things from your past, they're not going to help you move forward into a better life.

You have to let go of your past so you can focus on your future!

Have you ever wondered why some people seem to have everything going for them, while others can't seem to catch a break?

The answer is that some people are able to use their past experiences as assets, while others allow their past experiences to become liabilities.

Are you stuck in the past, or are you struggling to get out of the past and into the now?

Shift your mindset and have the courage to embrace the future and enjoy a more fulfilling life. Define your purpose and the strong reason why to move on with a better life.

**Action Points.** Steps for moving on for good from the past:

1. **Decide to actively let go of the past, accept attachment and make it a Must.** Identify the reasons holding you back and stay committed to letting go of the past.

2. **Change your emotional habits.** Perform a deep emotional introspection, identify the emotional habits and shift toward a more positive experience.

3. **Focus on right state of Mind.** Cultivate a mind of powerful thoughts, focusing on positive assets.

4. **Establish powerful rituals.** Establish new daily routines. Love yourself and your life, be grateful for what you have in your current life.

5. **Create your Life. Shift Your Focus.** Turn the negatives into the positives, setbacks into opportunities, failures into lessons and focus your actions and decisions you control for a life you deserve.

6. **Be Mindful of the Present.** Be engaged with your real life. Create more happiness and fulfillment.

7. **Create a Personal Growth Plan.** Identify areas for learning and improvement, pinpoint obstacles and assemble the tools to succeed.

8. **Elevate positive relationships.** Surround yourself with positive people committed to growth and progress.

9. **Serve Other.** Improve your life by giving, share with others the secret of living.

3

# The Secret to Make Patterns Work for You

Did you find yourself cycling through an unsuccessful pattern over and over again? The time has come to interrupt it in favor of a new, useful way of coping!

We all have patterns in our lives, make pattern work for you rather than against you.

These patterns can carry positive or negative connotations depending on how they affect your life. Patterns can also create self-fulfilling prophecy.

Patterns are repetitive behaviors that repeat themselves over time and are often used as a way to help us process information or make decisions quickly.

In this chapter, we'll discuss how to extricate yourself from those patterns that aren't serving you and use them in a way that will help you achieve your goals instead.

The first step is recognizing what patterns are and how they affect your life.

Patterns are not always bad, but when they become too ingrained in your life, they can cause more harm than good.

Your brain recognizes these patterns as something familiar and safe because it has seen this situation before and knows what response will work best at this time; however, sometimes these patterns become so ingrained in our brains that they begin working against us instead.

When you find yourself in a cycle of negative thinking or behavior, it can be difficult to break free. You may feel like you've tried everything and nothing seems to work.

**Action Points.** Steps to change your mindset and get out of repetitive behavior:

1. Recognize that the pattern exists.
2. Identify what triggers it and why you've been so resistant to change it before now; often times there are reasons for this resistance that are not always obvious at first glance (for example: fear).
3. Take action by making small changes each day until your mindset shifts enough for larger ones down the road (this could mean starting small with simple affirmations or visualizations before moving on to more complex exercises).

4

# Know Yourself. Live a Cohesive Life

I f you've ever felt as if there's something wrong with you or that no one understands what it's like to be in your shoes, then this chapter is for YOU!

Self-awareness is the foundation of everything you do. It's the first step in extracting your emotional self from a situation and learning how to live a cohesive life.

Learn how to master your perception of yourself and the world around you so that you can live a better life.

To truly transform your life, you need to be able to recognize when change is needed and then make it happen. Change is about shifting our perspective and making conscious decisions about how we define ourselves.

If you want to master change, you need to understand your personal assets and liabilities, so that you can use them for good.

Using your personal assets will help you overcome challenges by making things better.

You may have some assets already—for example, maybe you're an excellent communicator or know how to build relationships with people who can help you succeed in life or business.

Other assets may be less obvious at first glance—maybe you have a great sense of humor or are extremely patient when dealing with difficult situations.

When it comes down to it, assets are what get us through life: without them we'd be lost!

So take some time today and think about what practices you can learn to become more self-aware.

**Action Points.** Steps to cultivate self-awareness, and keep moving forward:

1. Understand and Recognize Emotions

- Recognizing your emotions helps you understand why you are having them and, in turn, how to regulate them.
- When you feel a certain emotion, ask yourself:

1. Where is this feeling coming from?
2. How did it make me feel emotionally, physically, or mentally?
3. How does this feeling make me feel like reacting?
4. How will this affect me and others later?

2. Pay Attention to Your Self-Talk

- Self-talk is the dialogue you have with yourself on a daily basis. The key to this is to simply start listening to what you say to yourself.
- Self-talk is forever occurring, even when you're not paying attention to what it is saying. There are many forms of self-talk: from self-limiting self-talk and jumping to conclusions to habits of speech and having others' thoughts becoming your own.
- Paying attention to these will help you understand the dialogue you have with yourself and the toll it takes on your emotions. It allows you to change it from negative self-talk to a more positive dialogue that can transform your physical, mental, and emotional health.

3. Practice Self-Evaluation

- Gain more insight by analyzing yourself, without judgment. Recognize and become aware of your weaknesses, strengths, habits, practices, relationships, goals, plans, values, and priorities that help guide you in the right direction.

## 4. Reflect

- Reflection allows you to notice patterns and understand your inner state. After adopting the first practice of recognizing, you can then start to reflect on what was recognized.
- One way to reflect is through journaling. Writing can help you process your thoughts, and create more headspace as you put your thoughts onto paper.
- Other ways in which you can practice reflection are by simply being still, and finding a quiet space where you can be alone with your thoughts.
- Meditation, yoga, and long walks are also wonderful options. Find a reflection practice that works best for you, and encourages you to keep practicing. By creating that space for yourself, you are making time to reconnect with yourself.

## 5. Practice Mindfulness

- The practice of paying attention to the present moment being experienced, intentionally and without judgment, is called mindfulness.
- It is the practice of being where you are, and observing what's going on inside and around us.
- Mindfulness can be done anytime, anywhere, and in a variety of ways. It may come in the form of noticing your footsteps you take, to savoring each bite of your meal, to an intentionally guided meditation session.

# 5

# Gain Perspective. Change Your Views of Circumstances

Do you want to have the answer to the life question "What I am going to do now?

Having perspective –being aware of the moment, using the past, understanding the present, and looking forward – offers a rational and thoughtful answer to life's eternal question.

The ability to see the world in all of its complexity is an asset that can be developed and strengthened over time.

Use perspective concept as a practical tool to:

1. Use time to gain intellectual perspective.
2. Obtain perspective and emotional clarity by analyzing pros and cons as well best – and worst-case scenarios.
3. Use change to achieve behavior perspective.
4. Become your own mirror, assess your perspective and see yourself as others see you.

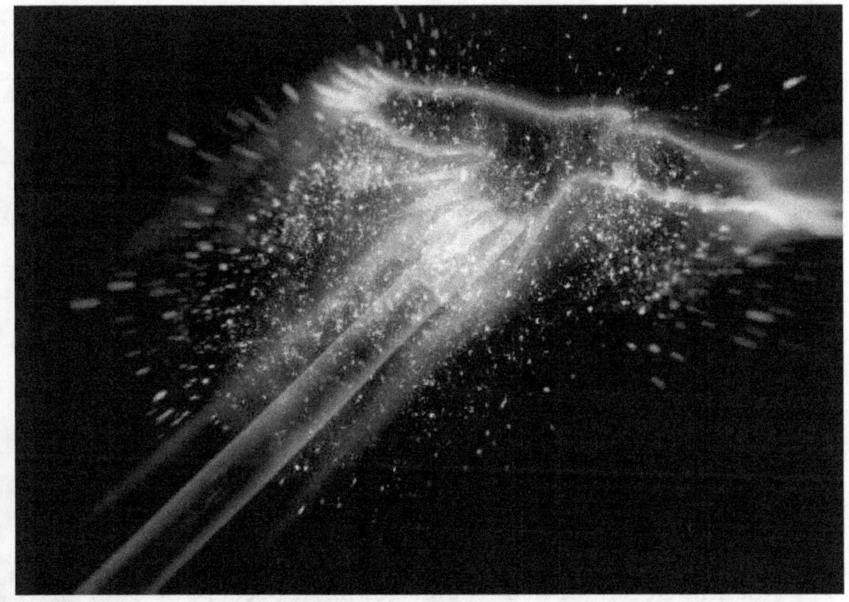

In one of previous chapters, we talked about how our minds naturally seek out patterns. This is a good thing! It helps us make sense of the world and make better decisions.

But when we're not aware of how our minds are doing this—when we don't have a clear picture of what's going on in our heads—we can find ourselves making decisions based on faulty logic.

Either way, these kinds of mental flubs can lead us down the wrong path if they aren't corrected quickly enough.

We might hear something one person says and think it applies to all people, so then we make a decision based on that assumption.

Or we might hear something someone else has said and think it applies to us specifically, so then we make a decision based on that assumption.

That's why it's important to remember that our brains are always trying to figure out where they fit into the world, or how they can change things for the better so that they feel like they belong somewhere safe and secure (which is why sometimes it feels like your brain is working against you).

People have viewed the world in history in different ways:

1. In ancient times, when people believed in a flat earth and believed that they were the center of it all, they had trouble seeing things from multiple perspectives. This led them to make bad decisions based on incomplete information.
2. When Columbus wanted funding for his journey across the Atlantic Ocean, he had trouble getting it because he didn't have enough evidence that there was another continent on the other side of the world. He had only seen one view—his own—of what lay beyond Europe's borders. It took him many years before his idea was accepted by others as possible truth rather than fantasy or myth (which is where it was left after earlier explorers had returned from their own expeditions).

The key to success **is** being able to see what others don't see—and this begins by changing the way you view the world.

**Action Points.** Assets-based thinking can be used to improve our perspective:

1. What could be or should be happening in any given situation.
2. Seeing people and situations as resources rather than liabilities.
3. Looking for solutions instead of problems.

4. Identifying hidden opportunities rather than obstacles.
5. Take a different approach toward problem solving and decision making so that instead of seeing issues as problems, they become opportunities for growth and innovation!

6

# Build Your Future. Set Goals

If you want your life to improve your life, you have to change your mindset, identify the problem and decide what it is that you need.

Once you do that, start working towards making that change happen. Identify the steps involved and then start taking them one by one until your goal is met.

The best way to overcome obstacles is to have a plan. Set goals and make them specific, so you can see what needs to be done, and then take action.

This may seem like common sense, but it's easy to feel overwhelmed when faced with a major problem or issue in your life.

It's tempting just to give up because it seems too big or complicated, but if you break things down into smaller parts and focus on solving those problems one at a time instead of trying to fix everything at once, then it will seem much less overwhelming!

Goal setting is one of the most important steps in life. It can also be one of the most difficult.

This is because goal setting is a two-part process: you need to have a direction, know what you want, and be specific about how you plan to get there.

When you try to solve problems without specificity, you end up making a lot of assumptions about what you are trying to accomplish—and as a result, you often don't even realize when your goals are out of reach or too expensive.

When you're specific about what you want, on the other hand, it's easier for you to gauge whether or not your goals are realistic and affordable. And with that knowledge in hand, it becomes easier for you to stay focused and motivated throughout the process of achieving them!

If you don't have a clear picture of your goal, it's easy to get lost in the details or get distracted by other things along the way.

It's important to keep your vision for yourself in mind as well as remember that sometimes, things don't work out exactly as planned.

That's okay! You can always adjust or try again until it works out just right.

Strategy is crucial in goal setting because it sets the stage for how you'll actually achieve your goals.

When you set out to achieve something, you need to have a strategy that helps us get there.

A well-defined strategy will help you stay on track and know when you're off course or need to adjust your approach.

This is especially important if you don't have experience with goal setting or reaching goals in general—you may not be used to having a clear plan of action.

In these cases, having a strategy can help you avoid getting stuck in an endless loop of trying different things until something works, only to find out later that it didn't work at all because something else was missing from your approach all along!

**Action Points.** Steps to set your personal long-term vision and short-term motivation goals that will raise your self-confidence:

1. **Set long-term goals** – what you want to achieve for your lifetime

as a broad and balanced coverage of all important areas in your life (family, financial, career, public service etc.).

2. Set **progressively smaller goals** – what you want to achieve in five-year, one-year and six - one month plan to help to reach the lifetime goals.

The **silver lining tips** to set effective and achievable goals:

1. The goals should have positive statements.
2. The goals should be precise and specific with measurable achieve-ments.
3. Set personal performance goals under your control.
4. Track, write the goals and review the outcome.
5. Set goals that you can achieve.

7

# "Lightning in a Bottle": The New Empowering Master System

I f you're reading this book, then you've probably been thinking about the changes you want to make in your life!

Whatever it is, we all have things we'd like to change about ourselves—and that's okay! The trick is figuring out how to turn these changes into reality.

With what I call "lightning in a bottle" tools you will begin to think in a more creative, and empowering way about change, see the big picture, listen to Universe Voice and determine what crucial skills you need in order to make a positive impact on your life.

You've heard the old saying, "If you don't like something, change it."

But how do you actually make that happen?

The light of silver lining you carry will help you transform your life and make the best of whatever change comes your way.

**Action Points.** Steps to determine what things mean to you and what you need to do about them in any situation in life:

1. See yourself in a new way, as someone who's not just struggling through a difficult situation but instead is working through it and making progress every day.
2. Listen for what the universe is telling you: what skills you need, what attitude will serve you best, and how to prepare for the changes ahead so they don't throw you off course.
3. Master change as an opportunity to make things better.
4. Prepare for change so that it doesn't catch you off-guard—and instead becomes a moment of opportunity for growth and expansion in your life.
5. Attitude is everything helps you navigate change and see the big picture.

And then? Then it's time to go out there and conquer!

# 8

# Achieve Positive Interactions

How do you reinforce the positive to achieve the satisfying interactions?

Interactions are a big part of life, and they're often very important. However, sometimes you find yourself in situations where there are challenges and obstacles to overcome.

When you are faced with these challenges and obstacles, it can be easy to feel like they are insurmountable. But they are not!

The key is to keep in mind that every interaction with others has a silver lining—you just have to be able to see it!

As you progress through life, you will encounter interactions that are both positive and negative.

The negativity can be damaging to your self-esteem and your relationships, where as the positivity is uplifting.

We are all different, and we all have our own unique ways of interacting with the world. But as we've discussed in previous chapters, change is possible.

It's not just about changing the way you see everything—it's about being able to control your own behavior and interactions with others.

The way we interact with others, including the way we treat ourselves, is vital to our happiness and well-being.

When you put yourself out there and act like a person who is positive and confident, others will be more likely to treat you well.

We all know that the way to make our lives better is by taking control of the things we can control. And one of the most important things we can control is our own behavior.

It's not always easy to do, though, especially when you're feeling stressed or overwhelmed.

Life is full of change: people come and go from your life, jobs come and go from your career path, and relationships come and go from your romantic life— and sometimes all at once!

With so many changes happening all at once, it's easy for you to feel overwhelmed by them all and just want everything else to stay exactly as it has always been.

But this attitude will only keep you stuck where you are right now, instead of getting you closer to where you want to be in life!

Interactions are also a great way to reinforce your own positive behaviors and beliefs, which is why it's so important to make sure that your interactions are positive as well!

**Action Points.** Steps to set yourself up for positive interactions:

1. **Practice empathy and understanding** - remember that everyone has their own story, and that everyone comes from a different place. Try your best to see things from their perspective, even if it goes against what you believe or think is true. This will help you avoid arguments, which can be draining on both parties involved!
2. **Acting with intentions** - build trust between people because it shows them they're being heard and understood by you. It also helps them feel more comfortable around you because they know that you're paying attention to them instead of somewhere else.
3. **Stay Connected** – use power of social interactions to empower health and wellness.
4. **Make Opposition Matter** – explore the possibility that opposing forces can both be true simultaneously. Create a new truth together!

9

# The Seven-Day Mindset Reset Challenge

Are you ready to turn your life right-side up?  Take control of your mind by not allowing yourself to hold any negative thoughts consistently.

Important rules to follow:

- **Rule 1**: No dwell on any unresourceful feelings or thoughts.  No disempowering questions or devitalizing metaphors.
- **Rule 2**: When begin to focus on the negative use problem-solving questions to redirect your focus towards a better emotional state.
- **Rule 3:** Set yourself up for success, establish empowering mental and emotional patterns each day in the morning for asking morning-power questions and in the evening using the evening-power questions.
- **Rule 4:** For the next seven consecutive days, the whole focus in life should be on solutions and not on problems.
- **Rule 5:** In case of backside, change immediately any unresourceful thoughts and start next day the seven day challenge over. The seven days consecutive program goal is not to hold any negative thought.

The **challenge** is very powerful and will bring benefits in your life:

1. Will help to identify all the mental habits that hold you back.
2. Make brain find powerful, helpful alternatives.
3. Give confidence to turn your life around.
4. Will create new expectations, and habits for a better life.

## Problem Solving Questions:

1. Identify what is great about the problem?
2. Ask what is not perfect yet?
3. What to do to make it in the way I want?
4. What am I willing to no longer do in order to make it the way I want it?
5. How can I enjoy the process while I do what is necessary to make it the way I want it?

## The Morning Power Questions:

1. What am I happy about in my life right now? What about that makes me happy? How does that make me feel?
2. What am I excited about in my life right now? What about that makes me excited? How that does makes me feel?
3. What am I proud of in my life right now? What about that makes me proud? How that does makes me feel?
4. What am I grateful for in my life right now? What about that makes me grateful? How that does makes me feel?
5. What am I enjoying most in my life right now? What about that do I enjoy? How that does makes me feel?
6. What am I committed to in my life right now? What about that makes me committed? How that does makes me feel?

7. Who do I love? Who loves me? What about that makes me loving? How does that make me feel?

## The Evening Power Questions:

1. What have I given today? In what ways have I been giver today?
2. What did I learn today?
3. How has today added to the quality of my life? How can I use today as an investment in my future?

# 10

# 360-Degree Life Self-Assessment

Improvement takes time be patient and persistent with your life journey.

Focus on the future and become a better you!

1. Identify areas for improvement in the major areas of your life.
2. Assess **Weekly / Monthly** the selected categories and rate (1 – 5) each area.
3. Set new goals and habits.
4. Evaluate the score and work on each areas of improvement for the next 30 days.

360 - Degree Life Self-Assessment Areas
Score (1=Low, 5=High)

1. **Health** (Evaluate all aspects of well-being)

2. **Relationships** (Assess quality of relationships in your life: family, friends, and love)
3. **Mental** (Cultivate joy, peace, positive energy and emotions)
4. **Experiences** (Experience life and special adventures, connections, interests, hobbies)
5. **Learning** (Discover new things and life around, develop personal skills)
6. **Financial** (Learn new skills, master the inner game of wealth, enjoy life earnings)
7. **Spiritual Life** (Connect with inner purpose, beliefs, faith and life values)
8. **Mission** (Contribute to the world, being engaged, fulfilled, energized, add value)

# 11

# Best Self Habits Assessment

Do you want to change your life and discover which habits you should improve?

Use Best Self Habits Assessment below to take control of your life :

1. Identify your high-performance habits.
2. Assess **Weekly / Monthly** the list and rate (1 – 4) each area of your life.
3. Set new habits for personal growth.
4. Evaluate the score and establish long-term strategies for improvement.

# 1. PRODUCTIVITY STRATEGY

## Score (1=Low, 4=High)

1. Focus on things that matter first
2. Track progress on major goals
3. Stay focused, avoid distractions
4. Set intentions on major activities
5. Stay fully engaged and enjoyed major efforts

# 2. BOOST ENERGY

## Score (1=Low, 4=High)

1. Approach the day with joy
2. Manage well energy level
3. Energize, recharge for the day
4. Increase physical workout
5. Balance life well being and sleep

# 3. POWER OF INFLUENCE

## Score (1=Low, 4=High)

1. Build connections and help others to grow
2. Listen and carry for others
3. Build a role model
4. Guide other on assets thinking
5. Build self-development

## 4. SHOW COURAGE EVERY DAY

Score (1=Low, 4=High)

1. Face difficulties heads-on
2. Challenge the status quo
3. Stand up for your values and beliefs
4. Take actions despite work required or risks
5. Share and be your authentic self with other

## 5. COMITTED TO NECESSITY

Score (1=Low, 4=High)

1. Practice your A-game
2. Share and affirm your daily 'why'
3. Improve emotional intelligence
4. Care and use gift to serve others
5. Accomplish tasks, meet deadline and finished duties

## 6. POWER OF GETTING CLARITY

Score (1=Low, 4=High)

1. Set a meaningful day
2. Act with intentions
3. Generate clear feelings
4. Stay focus on planned activities
5. Identify areas for self improvement

# 12

# Conclusions

We all have **a** silver lining. It's there, waiting for you to discover it, and once you do, it can transform your life!

Many people are afraid of change and don't know how to go about finding their own personal silver lining.

It's important to remember that change is constant—it's happening all around you every day. You can't avoid change or pretend it doesn't exist; you just need to be prepared for it when it happens so that you can use it as an opportunity instead of letting it get in your way.

There are many obstacles in life that can make it difficult to move forward. It's not always easy to see past these obstacles, but there are ways to do this.

Once you have learned life skills and gained experience with problem solving, it will be easier for you to recognize when something needs fixing.

Get out of the past and start problem solving so that things don't seem overwhelming anymore! This will involve recognizing obstacles and learning life skills, as well as seeing options for each day that comes your way.

You have to be willing to **t**ake the first step, but after that, you'll have to continue taking steps forward in order to achieve success.

This can be hard when you're faced with challenges and difficulties along the way—the more difficult it becomes to move forward, the more tempting it may seem to stop moving altogether. But if you keep going and stay focused on your goal, you'll eventually reach it!

Take control of your life, see the light of silver lining, get unstuck, use the power of change and transform your life to become a better version of YOU!

www.ingramcontent.com/pod-product-compliance
Lightning Source LLC
Chambersburg PA
CBHW060923130726
48001CB00006B/2382